SIDE

EFFECTS

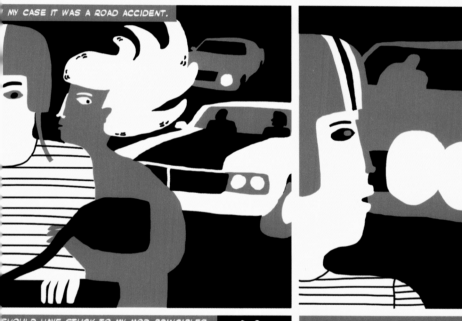

HEY RAYMONDO, LET'S GO INTO TOWN.

I WAS GETTING STONED EVERY SINGLE DAY.

LET'S GO BACK TO THE FLAT. I CAN'T HANDLE THIS.

YEAH. LET'S SPLIT.

GOING TO CROSS OVER. GOT TO GET OUT. HELL. WHO'S THAT COMING AT ME?

THIS IS AWFUL, WHY DON'T THEY LEAVE ME ALONE? I'VE GOT TO GET AWAY. GOT TO GET BACK.

JUST THREE MORE DOORS THEN I'M SAFE.

USSA ROAD

AT CHRISTMAS IN 1974, MY FATHER GOT ME ADMITTED TO HELLINGLY HOSPITAL, AN ASYLUM IN EAST SUSSEX.

THE PSYCHIATRIST SAID THERE WAS NOTHING WRONG. BUT I COULDN'T GO HOME. THERE WAS NOWHERE ELSE TO GO.

I WAS NICKED FOR STEALING PETROL AND SENT BACK TO HELLINGLY WITH A CRIMINAL RECORD.

THIS WAS THE START OF MY TIME IN THE REVOLVING DOOR.

BLOODY TRAFFIC AGAIN.

I'LL COUNT ALL THE CARS OVER FIVE MINUTES THEN AGGREGATE THE FIGURE.

I'M SURE THERE'S A TRANSMITTER IN HERE. THAT'S WHY THE TRAFFIC HAS BEEN FOLLOWING ME AROUND.

LATER, IN THE PSYCHIATRIST'S OFFICE.

HOW ARE YOU FEELING?

I'VE BEEN COUNTING THE CARS THAT COME INTO THE HOSPITAL.

RAY, WE THINK YOU HAVE SCHIZOPHRENIA. THERE IS A MAGISTRATE'S ORDER STIPULATING THAT YOU MUST RECEIVE ANTIPSYCHOTIC MEDICATION.

ABOUT 3,000 GO UP AND DOWN THE DRIVE EACH DAY. IS THAT REASONABLE?

ONCE A FORTNIGHT I HAD TO DROP MY TROUSERS AND HAVE SOMEONE INJECT MY BACKSIDE.

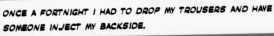

MEDICAL ROOM

NEXT ONE'S IN A FORTNIGHT AS USUAL. THERE'S NO INDUSTRIAL THERAPY TODAY AS IT'S THE SILVER JUBILEE DISCO.

FOR A WEEK AFTER THE INJECTION, I WOULD SUFFER A HORRENDOUS SIDE EFFECT CALLED AKATHISIA. AKATHISIA, FROM THE GREEK FOR "NOT TO SIT", REFERS TO INNER RESTLESSNESS CHARACTERISED BY AN INABILITY TO SIT STILL OR REMAIN MOTIONLESS.

CRIKEY, SHE'S NOT ONLY GORGEOUS, SHE'S GOT QUITE A REPUTATION.

HELLO... WHY DON'T YOU COME AND SIT WITH ME?

OH GOD, I FEEL DREADFUL.

DO YOU FEEL LIKE GOING SOMEWHERE?

GOT TO KEEP MOVING, CAN'T HELP IT.

VON HINTEN REIN! HEH HEH!

MALCOLM WAS A LAND MARINE AFTER D-DAY IN FRANCE. HIS JOB WAS TO GO OUT AFTER DARK WITH A FLAME THROWER AND FIND AND ATTACK GERMANS WHERE THEY SLEPT.

THAT'S DONE.

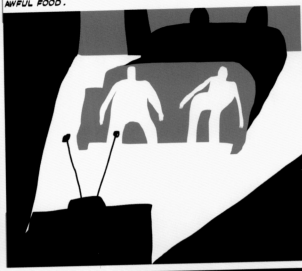

MANY ASPECTS OF ASYLUM LIFE I COULD ACCEPT, LIKE SLEEPING IN A TEN-BED MALE DORMITORY, THE LACK OF PRIVACY, THE AWFUL FOOD.

BUT THE INJECTIONS WERE HELL.

C'MON NOW SOLDIER MURPHY, SIT UP AND DRINK THIS COFFEE.

I CAN'T SISTER, THAT'S WHERE IT HURTS.

ONCE A DAY WE WERE SENT TO INDUSTRIAL THERAPY.

FRUIT CAKE?

NOT FOR ME MATE.

YOU KNOW CHRIS ALL THIS UNEMPLOYMENT IS WRONG. IT'S UNNECESSARY. IF THE GOVERNMENT SPENDS ENOUGH MONEY THROUGH BORROWING OR RUNNING A DEFICIT, UNEMPLOYMENT WILL GO DOWN LIKE IN THE 1960S.

IS THAT WHAT THEY CALL INDUSTRIAL THERAPY?

WE'VE HAD OVER 25% INFLATION SINCE 1979. UNEMPLOYMENT AND INFLATION ARE SUPPOSED TO BE MUTUALLY EXCLUSIVE

YOU CAN'T HAVE YOUR CAKE AND EAT IT.

COME ON, YOU KNOW WE START AT TWO. WE WANT A HAND LOADING THESE. RAY YOU CAN GO BACK TO PACKING SOAP.

BUT THESE WEREN'T JOBS TO HELP US. THEY WERE JOBS FOR THOSE RUNNING THE SYSTEM THAT KEPT PATIENTS WITHOUT HOPE OF INDEPENDENCE.

IT'S NOT THAT I MIND DOING THIS, BUT I WISH THEY'D STOP THOSE PEOPLE SHOUTING DOWN AT ME FROM PASSING AIRCRAFT.

I CAN GET SOME SOAP AND BACCY NOW.

WAGES, EVERYONE.

SALARY £1.75

THEN TO SEE THE NURSE.

I HATE THE AKATHISIA I GET WITH THESE INJECTIONS, NURSE.

AT THE WARD ROUND YESTERDAY THE DOCTOR SAID WE CAN LOOK AT DISCHARGING YOU. SO YOU'LL NEED TO GET A JOB.

I'VE STUDIED TO DEGREE LEVEL IN THE PAST.

WHAT DID YOU STUDY?

MARXIST IDEOLOGY AND THE ORIGINS OF THE COLD WAR.

THIS IS 1980. THINGS HAVE MOVED ON. YOUR STEP DAD AND THE CONSULTANT WANT YOU TO DO TYPEWRITER MECHANICS.

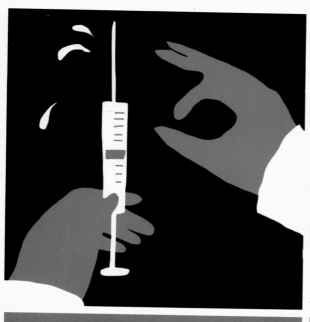

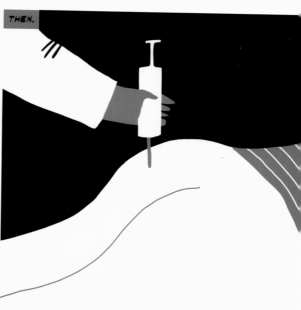

THEN.

OK, HERE'S THE NEXT TEST. THIS TYPEWRITER WEIGHS ABOUT FOUR KILOS. I WANT YOU TO CARRY IT UP THOSE STAIRS.

THAT'S RIGHT. NOW BRING IT DOWN AGAIN. WATCH YOU DON'T FALL.

LOOK OK TO YOU?

PUT HIM DOWN FOR THE NEXT TYPEWRITER MECHANICS COURSE.

THE SERIOUS BUSINESS OF TRAINING BEGAN. THERE WAS INSTRUCTION, APPOINTMENTS, THEN HOME LEAVE ON A BRITISH RAIL TRAVEL WARRANT.

ADJUST...LOOSE DOG... REMINGTON... FIXED DOG... ADJUST... BROTHER...BLAH

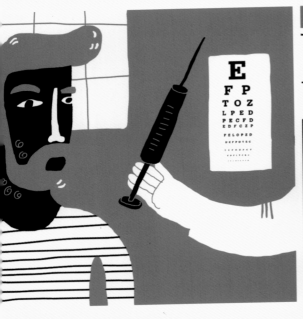

MR VOYCE, NURSE WANTS TO SEE YOU. ADLER...BLAH...LOOSE DOG...BLAH

I'VE HAD IT WITH THESE INJECTIONS. THEY GIVE ME A WEEK OF HELL AFTER EACH ONE.

DOCTOR'S WRITTEN YOU UP FOR INJECTIONS BECAUSE THEY DO YOU GOOD.

WHAT IF I REFUSE?

WELL YOU'RE NOT UNDER SECTION, SO I SUPPOSE THERE'S NOTHING I CAN DO.

RIGHT, THAT'S IT. I'VE HAD ENOUGH AND I'M NOT HAVING ANY MORE INJECTIONS.

WEEKS PASSED AND MY MENTAL HEALTH DETERIORATED.

THE IRA COULD BE LURKING IN HERE.

I WAS TERMINATED FROM THE TYPEWRITER MECHANICS COURSE AND SENT BACK TO LIVE WITH MY MUM AND STEPDAD.

I FEEL GREAT! HARDLY NEED TO SLEEP AND I'M SO ALERT!

I BUY SOME PAINT TO MAKE MORSE CODE SIGNS ON TREES AND SEE JESUS ON A CARNIVAL FLOAT.

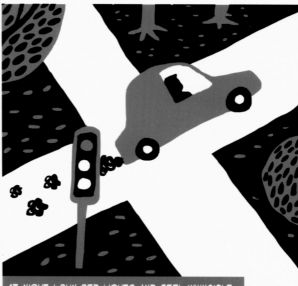

AT NIGHT I RUN RED LIGHTS AND FEEL INVINCIBLE.

PEOPLE TO SEE YOU, RAY.

WE THINK IT WOULD BE GOOD IF YOU CAME INTO HOSPITAL.

WHY SHOULD I? I'M NOT MAD. YOU CAN'T FORCE ME.

I'M AFRAID WE CAN. DR PATEL AND I HAVE SIGNED PAPERS TO SECTION YOU UNDER THE MENTAL HEALTH ACT.

DESPITE THE FUTILITY OF THE EMPLOYMENT PROGRAMMES, I'D ALWAYS BE A MODEL PATIENT AND EVENTUALLY GET MYSELF DISCHARGED.

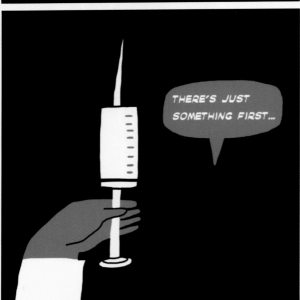

FIVE WEEKS LATER.

SO I'M HERE. I'VE SEEN THOSE THINGS AT SEA. I KNOW THE THIRD REICH IS STILL ALIVE. THERE ARE FORCES AT SEA AND A GIANT VESSEL FILLING THE WHOLE ATLANTIC. AND WHO KNOWS WHAT'S GOING ON IN DEEPEST SIBERIA. THIS IS WHAT THE COLD WAR IS ABOUT!

MAYBE THERE'S A GIANT CONSTRUCTION, THE RESULT OF A HUGE CONVEYOR BELT AND GIANT EARTH MOVERS, THAT REACHES INTO OUTER SPACE.

MAYBE MY CELL IS AT THE FOOT OF THIS HUGE MOUND THROWN UP INTO SPACE BY THE SOVIETS. SOMEWHERE NO ONE GOES, WITH UNFORTUNATES FALLING FROM THE TOP.

THE COLD WAR ISN'T ABOUT INTER-CONTINENTAL BALLISTIC MISSILES. WE'RE ALL BEING MOVED AROUND FROM ONE REALITY TO ANOTHER.

AFTER A COURT APPEARANCE, I WAS GIVEN A CONDITIONAL DISCHARGE. MY HOUSE WAS REPOSSESSED, SO HOMELESSNESS ARRIVED.

THIS IS SO MUCH BETTER THAN LIFE IN AN ASYLUM, WITH THOSE DEBILITATING INJECTIONS.

I KNOW I HAVE A HYPNOTIST WHO PUTS ME TO SLEEP THEN KEEPS ME WARM. THAT'S WHY I DON'T FREEZE TO DEATH.

FIVE YEARS LATER, IN THE GROUNDS OF OAKWOOD HOSPITAL.

MAKES A CHANGE FROM BUS SHELTERS. ONE LAST ROLL UP.

THE HEATING'S KEPT ON ALL NIGHT IN HERE. NICE AND WARM AND I CAN MAKE MYSELF A CUP OF TEA.

occupational therapy

DON'T MOVE AND THE DOG WON'T BITE.

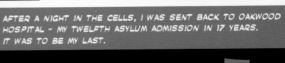
AFTER A NIGHT IN THE CELLS, I WAS SENT BACK TO OAKWOOD HOSPITAL - MY TWELFTH ASYLUM ADMISSION IN 17 YEARS. IT WAS TO BE MY LAST.

SO YOU ARE UNDER SECTION. I AM GOING TO PUT YOU ON DEPOT INJECTIONS.

WHY INJECTIONS? THEY GIVE ME HORRENDOUS SIDE EFFECTS! I'VE NEVER REFUSED TO TAKE TABLETS!

NO. I THINK WE PUT YOU ON DEPOTS.

NO! I'M NOT GOING THROUGH THIS ANYMORE! I'VE BEEN A REVOLVING DOOR PATIENT FOR 15 YEARS AND I WON'T TAKE THAT TORTURE AGAIN.

ONE OF THE TOOLS I'VE FOUND MOST CATHARTIC IS NARRATIVE. AT DIGITAL ART CLASSES, I BEGAN MAKING CARTOONS ABOUT MY DIFFICULT PAST.

THE READING IS FROM MARK'S GOSPEL, CHAPTER FIVE.

HERE IS ACCEPTANCE BACK AT CHURCH.

NOW I'M GOING TO SHOW YOU HOW TO DRAW PROFESSIONAL-LOOKING SPEECH BUBBLES.

IF ISSUES AFFECT YOU, WRITE THEM DOWN, DRAW THEM, SING THEM OUT.

NOW MEDICATION IS THERAPY, NOT TORTURE AND HUMILIATION.

RECOVERY IS NOT ABOUT A CURE OF AN ILLNESS OF A BIOLOGICAL ORIGIN.

YOU KNOW JOHN, I WORKED IN THREE GARDENS IN THE PAST AND EACH TIME I'VE BEEN FIRED AND ENDED UP IN THE LOONY BIN.

DON'T WORRY, YOU'VE BEEN HERE A FEW YEARS. YOU'RE OK.

THE END